COLIN GREENWOOD   HOW TO DISAPPEAR   A PORTRAIT OF RADIOHEAD

JOHN MURRAY

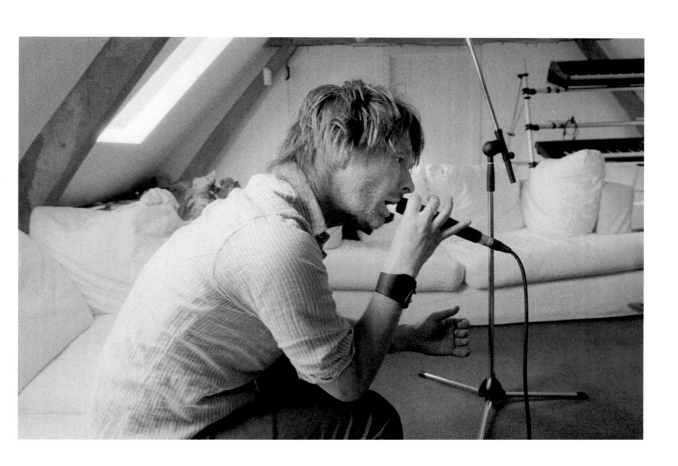

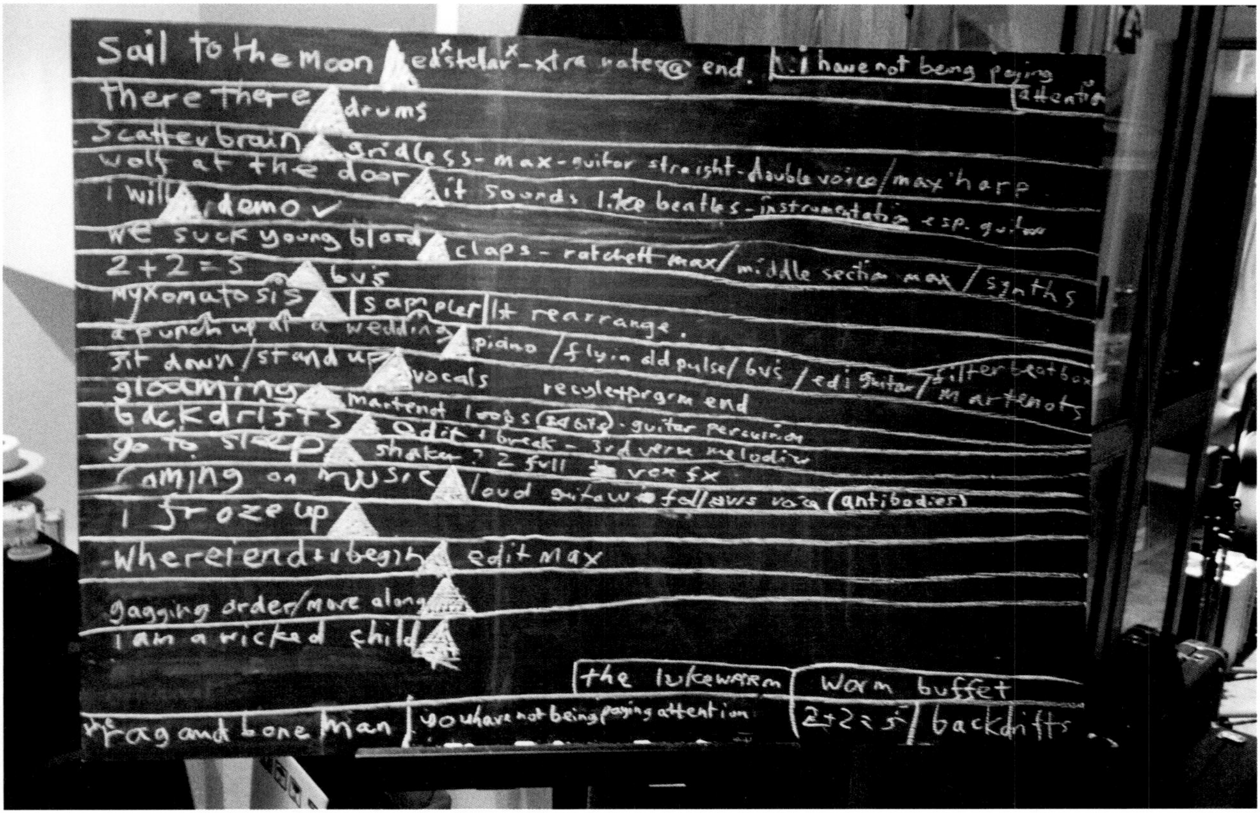

sail to the moon
there there drums
scatterbrain gridless - max - guitar straight - double voice / max harp
wolf at the door it sounds like beatles - instrumentation esp. guitar
i will demo
we suck young blood claps - ratchett max / middle section max / synths
2+2=5 bvs
myxomatosis sampler 1st rearrange.
a punch up at a wedding piano / fly in old pulse / bvs / edit guitar / filter beatbox
sit down / stand up vocals
martenot loops recycle prgrm end martenots
backdrifts edit + break - 3rd verse melodic guitar percussion
go to sleep shaker ? 2 full vox fx
loud guitar follows voice (antibodies)
i froze up
where i end + u begin edit max
gagging order / move along
i am a wicked child
the lukewarm
warm buffet
rag and bone man
you have not being paying attention
2+2=5
backdrifts

Fugitive Snaps

Most of these photographs were taken from 2003 onwards, when Radiohead had already found success with *OK Computer* and *Kid A/Amnesiac*. They chart our middle years: all the joy and doubt and confidence and uncertainty we would oscillate between, like many bands.

The perspective is uniquely my own: fugitive snaps born out of a shared world – we met at school and have remained together ever since. I have spent nearly all my working life either on stage or tucked away in a recording studio, where I've tried to catch out my friends with my Yashica T4 Super camera, a black analogue plastic box that records light, like our vinyl does sound.

We see very little of each other outside the cycles of recording and touring, and when we do reunite, it's like plunging into the latest season of a long-running box set: everything essentially the same but all of us just that little bit older. Thanks to our brilliant producer and old friend Nigel Godrich, some of the studios we have recorded in have been 'pop-up' affairs: mixing desks and tape machines wheeled into plush Hollywood homes, or abandoned English country houses redolent of ruined Saltburns. The simple choices that once bound us together when we were starting out have, over time, been changed by the complicated branches and tributaries of our lives apart. Coming back together at these moments is both addictive and reassuring – a communion through music.

When we are with each other, much of the time is spent waiting in anticipation – to rehearse, record, travel, play concerts – shuffling between these states over and over. Sometimes I would photograph during the endless downtime, when we were often all quite bored, trapped in airless back rooms for hours on end, falling into time-killing coping routines: crossword puzzles, snoozing, reading or, me, just bothering other people.

I am inspired by some of the great photographers, just as musically I strive to emulate my bass heroes. Tim Barber's 2005 website, Tiny Vices, has been an important influence: an online gallery before the days of Instagram containing images sent to him from all over the world –

snaps of small pleasures, photos of friends, road trips documented with 35 mm cameras like mine – beautifully curated with an expert eye. From him I learnt how to make an event out of a casual image. I met him once in New York, and it was he who recommended the Yashica camera I've used for much of this book.

I would also experiment with different cameras, finding new ways to capture the moment, trying to fill the frame with what felt vital in that instant. I'm interested in photographs purely as evidence, forensic records of how we worked and changed a space: closed-off barns, those run-down country houses, empty arenas. And while performing, I would have a couple of cheap plastic cameras on standby, sitting on top of my Ampeg SVT amplifier and 8 x 10-inch speaker cabinet, ready to grab when I could take my hands off my guitar. Typically, the bass travels through the whole of a song, but with much of our music there are pauses and spaces in my bass lines, where I drop out and come back in. Dead centre at the back of the stage, flanked by Clive, our second drummer for some of these years, and Phil – two bald men fighting over a bass player – I would seize these opportunities. All the sound and light that enveloped us would distract the others from my camera, offering up moments of candour and unselfconsciousness.

Once, I remember Thom holding up a crystal Jason Evans had brought along to a professional shoot he was doing, as part of his experiments with the distortion and refraction of light waves into his camera lens. It struck me that he was attempting something similar to our manipulation of sound waves: slowing them down, delaying and separating, fuzzing the edges. Sometimes, on stage, Andi Watson's lights would burn out parts of the image I was attempting to capture during songs. I learnt to be grateful for these happy accidents and to welcome them.

One of my regrets is that I haven't been bolder with the lens, got closer, taken more photographs. I'm shy with a camera. But I'm not there to take pictures and sometimes I find it tricky to navigate the distinct roles of musician and photographer. I try not to wander about the stage like a lost tourist. You're arranging the frame, searching for the revealing moment, that impulse to press the shutter release before both feeling and image are lost in the onrush of sensation, of sound, smoke and light. It can feel intrusive and disruptive to step in and record a collective experience when you are part of the group that is striving to be *in* that moment. Especially shooting people who are wary of that process. The others have mostly been tolerant of my snapping, but my brother has embraced it. If you're looking for the book 'Jonny Greenwood: My Life in Rock', I've got that. There are probably more pictures of him than anyone else here: he was the happiest to be in front of the camera by far. Perhaps as his big brother, I could boss him about.

Early Days

We were all at the same small independent school in Abingdon, just south of Oxford. I was unhappy there until sixth form, when I found I could escape into the academic and extra-curricular sides of things: literature and the band. The music department was run by an inspirational director, Terry James, who was also my neighbour in a small close near RAF Abingdon. I remember him once emerging from his front door across the road, sleeves rolled up, his arms and hair white with flour from making bread. Years later, when he'd retired, and we were playing an arena near Cardiff, he came to see the show and afterwards gave us a lesson in the dressing room, generously comparing our music to the early twentieth-century French composer Francis Poulenc. I went straight out and bought all the Poulenc I could lay my hands on. I loved its bright melodic invention but couldn't quite see its connection to us. It was typical of Terry, though – a flattering kindness, always keen to share his love of music. One time, I remember we rehearsed on a Sunday at the school, and the next day the headmaster sent us a bill for £60. Perhaps we disturbed his weekend. Terry took the bill back to the HM's office, tore it in half and left it on his desk.

We would rehearse constantly, but never play any gigs. I must've booked most of the village halls in south Oxfordshire for our band practices. My brother and I were too young to drive, so we'd pile into Ed's little yellow Fiat or Phil's white Volkswagen Beetle. At the beginning, playing in the band was more about companionship and access to a different age group – Phil and Ed were in years above us. Rehearsals became a comforting haven of shared jokes and conversations that helped soften the sharp shifts and long boredoms of teenage years.

The first gig I played was at a drunken sixth-form party thrown at a rugby club in west Oxford, with Ed and Thom and a drum machine. The first gig with my brother was at the underground Rock Garden, now a gleaming glass-and-brick Apple store in Covent Garden. Jonny didn't play guitar then, just the keyboards and a penny whistle. I'd forgotten to bring a stand, so he had to perform his first ever show with his synth propped on an amplifier, his back to the crowd of friends we'd brought along from Oxford. I'd like to think that, if we'd been American, we'd have been playing late-night shows in crammed bars, before going on to record into the small hours, like my Motown and Memphis heroes. In fact, we hardly played in public at all, and spent long summer holidays and half-terms cloistered away in all those echoey village halls, setting up our gear between toddler groups and coffee mornings, practising among the peeling crash mats and kids' chairs.

Our first proper shows were in a small pub venue in Oxford, the Jericho Tavern. We played there a few times in the summer of 1991, culminating in a concert that autumn when thirty-odd A&R people came from London to see us. Mac, the promoter, sound-mixer and curator of the local music scene, made them all pay. Being a performer on a tiny stage with the audience almost on top of you, as well as being part of that audience supporting the opening artists before going on, is a connection I try to keep even though we now play more detached spaces. To this day, I still wander the crowd in the build-up.

By the end of 1991, we had managers and a recording contract with EMI, signed by a man called Nick Gatfield who had played with Dexys Midnight Runners. It's his saxophone on 'Come On Eileen'. Metallica and Nirvana were very big, and perhaps EMI thought they might be getting some kind of mishmash of that with us.

I remember taking the bus up to the EMI offices on the corner of Manchester Square in London, famous for The Beatles and the Sex Pistols, and being ushered into a boardroom to meet the head of the company, Rupert Perry, snug in a Christmassy jumper and cradling a mug of coffee. He told us that we wouldn't see him again unless we sold lots of records, a reverse ransom of sorts. Then we got the bus back home to Oxford, where some of us went off to the pub in the rain to celebrate.

My First Bass

When we started as kids, my classical-guitar lessons in my back pocket, I didn't imagine that the bass would be my role. But Ed already had a guitar, so I was asked to play bass. Someone from Stereolab once said something about the bass which stuck with me: how it is the bridge linking the melody of voice and guitar with the rhythm of the drums. During the sessions for our first album, *Pablo Honey*, Paul and Sean, our American producers for 'Creep', would shout at me, 'You are the glue!'

Music that has the bass as its essence has always been a deep influence on me. I had a small Toshiba mono cassette player, a birthday present and my gateway into songs at the age of thirteen, which I would listen to obsessively, reaching into the sound coming from the tiny 3-inch speaker for the low-end melody – albums by Joy Division, The Fall, Cocteau Twins. I adored old soul, especially Otis Redding. I learnt how to play along to Donald 'Duck' Dunn's melodic, driving bass lines that tethered Redding's huge, yearning vocals to the in-house Stax sound of Booker T's band. Lots of post-punk records from my older sister schooled me too, especially Joy Division's *Unknown Pleasures* with Peter Hook's prominent bass, and the even more tune-packed lines he played with New Order and their journey into dance and sequenced rhythms.

The first bass I owned was a black Westone Spectrum DX. My mum bought it for me. She always encouraged Jonny and me to spend time dedicated to music. I loved that Westone, of course, but once we had a deal and could afford more instruments, I dropped it for an expensive black Ernie Ball Music Man StingRay (lots of nineties indie bands were using them, like Curve and Ride). My forsaken Westone ended up being used as a doorstop at our management's office.

The Music Man bass had a battery inside which lent it a growling, zingy sound that could cut through all the other instruments. But it felt too brash and new to me. Later, I would own a beautiful dark-green 1976 StingRay, one of the first of its kind. A friend in an American band we toured with, The Werefrogs, sold it to me on condition I'd sell it back to him if I ever tired of it. It was just the deepest and most soulful-sounding bass I've ever had. I loved that bass. I only recorded one song with it – 'Lucky' on *OK Computer* – before it was stolen along with all our instruments from outside a motel close to Denver airport, in 1995. If anyone in Colorado reading this knows anything, I'd still like it back. We were on tour supporting Soul Asylum at the time, and had to drive over a thousand miles to Black Market Music in San Francisco, where we re-stocked. Back then you could walk in off the street and buy incredible old guitars, before the advent of eBay made them easy pickings as investments for wealthy businessmen. I chose a battered, heavy old 1976 Fender Precision in tobacco sunburst, the bass lots of my heroes like Dunn and Motown's James Jamerson played.

I've bought others too, including a 1960s Precision from Nashville, Tennessee. Scraped up and bruised, with a sunburst finish and a cracked, orange-flecked scratch plate, it came with a letter explaining it was once used in Steve Earle's band. That bass wants to be played in the studio and on stage – it just sings. Recently, I performed at the Ryman Auditorium with Nick Cave, accompanying him across America while he reshaped his incredible songbook into an intimate show for bass, piano and voice. Ryman's was for a time the home of the original Grand Ole Opry in Nashville, a stained-glass meeting house with banks of wooden pews for seating, inspired by old tabernacles and places of worship. Playing on that stage inspired me to look for a bass that was part of that rich culture.

Recording Studios

In 1988, Ed and Thom called Chipping Norton Recording Studios from a red telephone box to ask about hiring it to record our demos. Formerly a Victorian schoolhouse, it had been converted into a professional residential studio, famous for Gerry Rafferty's 'Baker Street'. Unfortunately, we couldn't afford the £900-a-day rate, so we worked at friends' houses and smaller studios instead. A few years later, we found that we were able to afford CNRS for *Pablo Honey*, and I remember the excitement of staying there, even if it was only twenty miles away from home. There was a neon jukebox that played scratchy 45s, old soul tunes like the O'Jays' 'Back Stabbers', that we'd mime to around the pool table. We'd wake up to a cooked breakfast before rushing into the studio. *Pablo Honey* was made by Sean Slade and Paul Q. Kolderie, two Bostonians who were responsible for some of our favourite records with artists like Buffalo Tom, the Pixies and Dinosaur Jr. I remember the first time that Thom and I went to pick them up from Oxford's Randolph Hotel in our rusty white van, the doorman wouldn't let us in.

Like Paul Jackson's footage of The Beatles rehearsing in Richmond, London, we would begin our sessions sitting in a circle with our instruments, drinking tea and chatting – the shared language and humour of friends who'd grown up together. With *Pablo Honey*, and particularly with *The Bends*, we were mainly finessing songs we'd toured endlessly across America. It was tough reshaping them into forms that would bear repetition on record, to give them a unique aura and quality that was distinct from the experience of them on the road. Of course, that comes from Thom's voice, and the treatment our songs were given by Sean, Paul, John Leckie and particularly Nigel Godrich.

Nigel has been by our side since we first worked with him on *The Bends*, when he was assisting John Leckie at RAK studios in St John's Wood, London. One day, while John was away mixing songs at Abbey Road, we recorded 'Black Star' with Nigel, which we had intended as a B-side. But he brought something to it, and we realised we had a song that deserved to be on the album. That gave us the confidence to work with him on *OK Computer*. Nigel settles on a 'balance' so quickly, allowing us to find the coherence and beauty in the songs we are constructing, all that explorative bashing and scraping in the live room with him next door behind the faders. He can make something out of anything, and with him the studio itself becomes another musical instrument in our armoury, changing the songs from documents of us playing together to something new we are excited to take back out into the world.

Our Own Studio, Dressing Rooms, America

Our Own Studio

Eventually, we were determined to build a studio for ourselves, close to home in Oxford. In 1999, we found a long barn in a small village on the Thames and converted it, ready to start work on recordings that would become *Kid A* and *Amnesiac*. It was a soaring space with chunky wooden spiral stairs and balustrades, an airy treehouse nestled inside an ancient English tithe barn. There was one high-vaulted room for writing and rehearsing, connected by big white double doors to its twin, a tall control room with a mixing desk and outboard gear. The control room was lavishly carpeted in thick ginger wool pile picked out by Thom and me at Allders department store in Oxford. Above that was a mezzanine floor, where Dan, who goes by the pen name Stanley Donwood, would come and work on images as the music played below.

From *The Bends* onwards, Dan has collaborated with Thom to create the artwork for all of our albums and merchandise; he is an important part of how we send our music out into the world. They first met at art school in Exeter.

At the other end of the barn, above a kitchen and sitting area, a short spiral of stairs led to a wooden room that became a second studio, a small project space with an old Neve mixing desk, vintage keyboards and white sofas tucked under the pitched eaves of the roof. There were bedrooms below that looked out onto a farmyard garden with raised beds for vegetables, an ancient orchard filled with damson and plum trees, golden quinces, sharp red Spartans, Bramleys and other old varieties of apple. I would make chutney, pies and membrillo paste from the quinces.

Tucked away at the back of the old farmyard was a row of cowsheds we converted into storage. Inside one of these we installed a massive wood-burning stove to warm a studio space for Thom and Dan to paint in. It had a rough dirt floor, and tiny worn wooden desks and chairs culled from the previous owner's career in teaching. After long periods away on tour, we'd finally get back home to write or rehearse and find gobbets of brightly coloured verminous turds on the painting shed's floor, from the rats and mice that had munched on Dan's discarded paint tubes.

While Nigel edited, or if the work became too focused and intense, I would sometimes escape there to sit with Dan while he scratched and scraped his acrylic paints on vast square canvases, early mixes of the music burnt on blank CDs playing on an old boom box in the corner. Watching him at work, seeing how the songs in utero would be inspiring him, has been a welcome distraction from the studio.

Dan cycles everywhere and would get to us by train from Bath with his big black bike on board. He has stayed with us on most of our recording adventures elsewhere, in those old, abandoned country houses. At Tottenham House in Wiltshire, on the edge of Savernake Forest, for the record *In Rainbows*, he pitched his Albion canvas festival bell tent on the back lawn behind the house's ha-ha. He warmed it with a small stove while we shivered in chilly caravans. Most recently, he joined us at La Fabrique studio in the South of France, for the *Moon Shaped Pool* sessions. He built some 5-foot square boxes, a foot deep, waterproofed them, filled them with water and oil pigments, and immersed enormous canvases in them, leaving the wind and weather to do the rest, swirling the paints onto the surfaces, a sort of massive marbling.

When we record, bass and drums are often the first instruments we lay down. Standing between two loudspeakers, playing along to Phil's rhythm track, I have the best seat in the house. I feel the same way on stage too, playing alongside Phil, staring up at him on his drum riser. On the *In Rainbows* tour, Phil was impeccably turned out in suits made by an old friend and former Savile Row tailor, David Clarke, who added extra fabric under his jackets' armpits, as he would have done for an orchestral conductor, for those swinging arms. Phil has always supplied a rhythm and a backbeat that has revealed the bass line to me as something natural, inevitable, pointing me towards the way to play in sympathy with Thom's singing. Sometimes the songs we record have first set sail with just Thom's voice and guitar; sometimes we have spent hours listening over and over to Nigel's backing tracks – when we made *OK Computer* at Jane Seymour's sixteenth-century manor house near Bath for example – absorbed in the beautiful sound picture he would cast from our playing, all the loops and samples spun out on metres of magnetic tape spooled on microphone stands across the control-room floor.

Many outstanding musicians have played on our records over the years, mostly to music arranged by my brother. From the first parts he wrote for *The Bends*, Jonny has brought new colours to our music, shaping the emotional temperature of the songs into a charged and dynamic whole, such as the string arrangements on 'How to Disappear Completely' and 'Pyramid Song'. On *Amnesiac*, Humphrey Lyttelton and his jazz band added a sad Dixie swing to 'Life in a Glasshouse'. In the same studio, RAK, Jonny wrote for all-female choral voices on *A Moon Shaped Pool*. The arrival of professional musicians in the studio puts us on our toes – there's a sense of wonderment and fear about how their contributions can be incorporated into the locked musical box we've already arrived at. We're searching for something to complete the experience of the song, reaching for aesthetic ideals that have informed us – Thom's love for Charles Mingus's *Town Hall Concert*, for example, with its wild rancorous horns peeling off each other, inspiration for the impromptu horn break in 'The National Anthem' on *Kid A*.

There's never been one overriding style we've all adopted and stuck to – our musical diet is catholic and disparate. We all bring music that inspires us to the studio. I remember Ed putting on 'I Am the Walrus' at Jane Seymour's house, the mixing desk and speakers in the library overlooking the long Jacobean garden, all that joy in the sound confected with the artifice of Abbey Road's nascent technology. Listening to that song, as we were about to lay down the first sessions for *OK Computer*, was both terrifying and inspiring.

I'll hear a piece of music, and it will trigger something, retrieve a moment from my musical memory palace – a style, a phrase, a mood or an arrangement. In my head, our music is a conversation with other musicians – for me Isaac Hayes is there in 'Weird Fishes/Arpeggi', Al Green is there in a live performance of 'Nude' in Tokyo. These responses are personal, and surely make no sense to anyone else. They are emotional accords between what we are performing and working on, and the musical journey I've taken to bring me into that moment.

Both these songs are on the A-side of *In Rainbows*, a record we started at Tottenham House. That place felt haunted to me, too creepy and structurally unsafe even to sleep in. It had been a post-war prep school with a subterranean gymnasium and derelict fly-strewn bathrooms filled with ranks of tiny, stained washbasins where the boys would brush their teeth. We worked in large empty state rooms overlooking a smashed and rusted orangery that had lost all its glass from a nearby American ammo-dump explosion after the war. I remember sitting on the stone steps behind the control room Nigel had built, playing along to Phil's drums on the frantic song 'Jigsaw', my back to the 24-track Otari tape machine, staring out at the brambles and briers wrapped around the contorted carcass of the glasshouse.

It was a cold October, and we slept in tiny caravans parked on the back lawn, ate in an enormous room of bare wood and plaster, where the money had run out before the walls could be marbled. The owners' ambition had foundered on the size of the house, and we sometimes wondered if in staking it out for our album we'd done the same to ourselves. Bikers would park up at the end of the long drive and stroll the sheep-filled parkland in their leathers, spreading out below the towering monument to King George III, scrutinising the grass, hunting for magic mushrooms. When we went back home for weekends, an asthmatic 'security guard' with a baseball bat patrolled our pop-up studio of consoles and racked guitars. We were only too happy to finally get back to our cosy Oxfordshire barn, where Nigel moved his gorgeous old Automated Processes, Inc. desk into the control room to mix those Tottenham House recordings.

The first time we recorded in America was 2003's *Hail to the Thief*, at Los Angeles' Ocean Way Studios on Sunset and Gower. In early January 2010, we returned to Los Angeles to continue recording *The King of Limbs*. This time, we all stayed and worked at Drew Barrymore's house, the same house above Sunset Boulevard that had once hosted The Beatles and Dean Martin, and that features in John Boorman's haunted, gangster revenge film, *Point Blank*. The sprawling, hazy beauty of our studio setting infused the music we were trying to make, which was less concerned with song structures and more about rhythms and textures: sound beds that would be inspiring enough for Thom to write and sing over. The screening room became our control room, and we set up a live room at the front of the house, with views overlooking West Hollywood below. Phil had his drums in a chandeliered formal room next door. After childhoods spent in grim 1970s England, the clean Californian light felt like a different world to us.

Growing up in an Oxfordshire close, I remember being entranced by the glossy escapism of the James Bond films and their gadgets, girls and guns. Amazing songs, too. In the nineties, we'd sometimes play Carly Simon's 'Nobody Does It Better' as an encore – you can find it on some dusty back page online. So, when Sam Mendes and Barbara Broccoli approached us to record the title song for *Spectre*, we jumped at the chance. They wanted something in the style of 'Pyramid Song'. With Thom's darkly beautiful lyrics and Jonny's swooping, melodic strings, 'Spectre' was recorded in the soaring space of Studio 1, Air Studios, Belsize Park, London. In the end, our song wasn't used in the film, so instead we released it as a Christmas present to fans. Since then, it's had a limited outing live. I hope we'll get to play it again one day, and with an orchestra too.

Dressing Rooms

Dressing rooms are liminal spaces, in-between worlds. The best can be RV wagons, circled around AstroTurfed mini-quadrangles with table football, ping-pong and fairy-lit slumber couches. The worst are thrown up behind massive sound systems on Flemish fields, flimsy sheds with rattling walls buffeted by gusts of bass from Major Lazer. At a festival, where lots of bands are gathered in cubicles, the wait to go on stage can feel like the anxious moments before a medical exam: the dread of an impending procedure in front of thousands of onlookers, other musicians too; an anxiety dream made real. We've spent a lot of time holed up underground, in the bowels of sports arenas and stadiums, cocooned locker rooms swagged off in heavy black drapes that

hide rows of hooks for kit, showers and ice baths. My brother loves to play his recorder and violin in these large, white-tiled communal bathrooms, for the bright reverb they give him. Time seems to concertina in these dressing rooms – you get there hours in advance, and then suddenly it's 8.30 p.m. and time to go on.

Arriving at a venue around lunchtime, we search for catering and the dressing room, long looping walks around the edge of the Smoothie King arena. The crew have been here since 5 a.m., erecting the stage and putting up the signage, colourful arrows in green and blue with Dan's teasing artwork of dark forests and jagged thorns: other worlds to be lost in. The riggers will be hard at work attaching the lights, crawling over the metal truss that flies high above the stage, like crew from an old clipper fixing sails across its raking masts. When we toured in 2008, there were stalactites of LEDs that formed a field of light above our heads, sweeping and glittering and dripping down diodes of colour; on the last tour a surfboard of lights bathed the stage in a soft diffuse glow. We've worked with Andi Watson, our lighting designer, for nearly as long as we've been performing and, never mind his empathetic understanding of our music, I wouldn't have had so much luck with my live photographs without his creative support.

But before all this, before the evening show, there are lots of hellos and how-are-yous, tea-making for the backline crew who are busy unpacking enormous flight cases stacked with ancient American guitars. I would wander through the vast empty arenas we played, ours for the night, marvelling as all the equipment was ferried from the shiny red-and-chrome Peterbilt trucks, tipped out of their boxes to be reassembled on vast metal stages, carefully wheeled into position on the arena floor beneath a jostling basket of flying speakers, spotlights, LED screens and mirror balls like dangling sputniks. There's a profusion of technical detail on stage that's masked in the darkness and shrouded in grey dust-cloths, like the memory of those mothballed country houses we recorded in. At the soundcheck I would stand at the heart of the stage, cradled by it all, crew technicians all around me making their final adjustments, others busy by the open racks of guitars in the wings. And at the end of each night, the crew in Radiohead T-shirts, colour-coded for lights, sound, etc., would herd the repacked boxes back into their trailers, wearing white hard hats like Nintendo characters in a massive Tetris game.

America

We'd always been inspired by English bands who went to America to play and stayed there for weeks, months even. Our first tour started in Boston, a hard town with music-sated crowds that fed into our jet-lagged fears on stage. But as we travelled further south and west, deeper into our American dream, we sloughed off our defensive English insecurities, and by the time we reached the golden West Coast and Los Angeles, we'd embraced our dream of playing music for life, in a country and culture that had nurtured us with its songs and stories.

On that early tour we travelled in the comfort of a super-wide silver bus with fluted aluminium panels, on the side a long airbrush portrait of a white stallion plunging through the ocean's surf. We'd arrive early in the morning at the club or art-deco theatre, at Deep Ellum in downtown Dallas perhaps, stumbling off the bus into the hard bright day, banging on the fire-escape doors to use the washroom before jumping in a cab to a motel room downtown. The clubs were in the cooler, looser parts of town, when zoning and police hadn't yet decided what to do with them, and we'd spend our downtime exploring coffee shops and small indie book and record shops, thrift stores selling vintage American styles we recognised from all the films. With that open American friendliness and courtesy that contrasted with the guarded formality back home, we'd be asked where we were from, what we were doing. In a band, we'd say, in our best BBC received pronunciation, playing tonight at the Chameleon Club on West Queen Street.

The sugar-rush success of 'Creep' in America probably saved us from being dropped by EMI and granted us grace to record *The Bends* in 1994, although that record was overlooked by many when it first came out, and some dismissed us as a one-hit wonder. I spoke to so many music writers who'd received *The Bends* as a promo, left it to gather dust on top of their PC tower, and hadn't bothered to play it until word of mouth nudged them. The slow-burn success of that record, and all the touring we did to support it, meant that when we released *OK Computer* three years later nobody wanted to make the mistake of missing out on us again.

In 1995 and 1998, we went to Japan, touring in the spirit of those clubs we'd experienced in America. We were keen for something more than just hit-and-run shows in the big cities. Everywhere we travelled we were followed by a small group of fans – I remember a snowball fight with them when our train to Nagano broke down in a blizzard. One night we might be playing a small hotel function room along the Hakata River in Fukuoka, the next a hall on the seventh floor of a high-rise in the compressed concrete and neon bustle of Tokyo's Shinjuku district. The jet lag was crippling at first, which Phil especially found challenging. Our record company there, Toshiba EMI, picked up on this, and together with some very excited Japanese fans, inaugurated the Phil Is Great Fan Club with a celebratory lunch of his favourite food: steak and potatoes. Phil, as ever, was the perfect host.

105

Arenas

The long, intimate incursions into America's heartland changed for us in 1995, when REM invited us to open for them. They were playing huge arenas and sports domes, with towering stages many times bigger than anything we'd experienced before. I remember our American Eagle tour bus rolling directly into the middle of the St Petersburg ThunderDome in Florida, like a child's Matchbox car lost under a kitchen table. The Dome, plastered with billboards for soft drinks and sports teams, was spanned by a colossal, curved roof with a tiny circle of light at its apex, where a collared dove flapped helplessly, trying to escape. All of REM's shows were at this type of out-of-town arena, ringed by parking lots (we'd later have bus barbecues and frisbee parties on them) that fed on to freeways. We would spend all day there in that stale air-conditioned microclimate, watching the thousands milling about the drinks concessions, terrifying and dislocating after the sweaty embrace of the clubs. But in time we were able to relax, and to play our songs differently, putting more space into the music that we sent out across those large dark caverns, sticking closely together on the vast carpeted stages.

We learned a lot from REM, who themselves had worked out how to scale up their performances for these bigger crowds. The whole feel of those shows became different, altering our connection with the audience. The travelling and backstage experience changed too, cloistered into something more hermetic, like a Covid bubble.

Touring is like taking your office with you every day, but instead of saying goodbye at 5 o'clock, you're travelling by bus from show to show, sharing a rolling dormitory with your co-workers. Waking up the next morning and making a first cup of tea at dawn, swaying in sympathy on a bus that's sailing through the Arizona desert, is one of the extraordinary romances of being on the road in America. We've criss-crossed the continent in American Eagles, and the boxier but bigger Prevost – floating through America's vast landscapes, playing bridge in the back lounge as we slow down and leave the freeway to Phoenix. The buses are configured to have a long front lounge, with sleeping bunks for up to twelve

in the middle section, names gaffer-taped to the glossy veneer. Everyone has their favourite bunk. I've found myself drifting towards the beds on top: it's quieter there. In England, the buses are more utilitarian, often with two decks, but with a more cramped sleeping area. There's a story that Elvis Costello once brought an American tour bus back to the UK, only for it to be sabotaged by a worried domestic coach firm, its petrol tank filled with sugar.

I love jumping buses from the band's to the backline crew's, where there's reggae and beer on ice in the back lounge, books and chess up front. In the morning, our guitar technician, Peter 'Plank' Clements, made tea and toast, and we would sit and stare out at the unending deserts and prairies, for hour after hour – the white fences of Midwest townships, the vast swathes of farmland all canopied in green – feeling gloriously cut adrift until shimmering skyscrapers appeared on the horizon, our next port of call.

In the early days, one of the first things we spent our tour support money on from EMI was flight cases, and we chose the colour purple, thinking it would be harder to mislay the heavy boxes on wheels when packing the rusty white van back to Oxford. We bought a battered outsize Volkswagen LT45 from a garage on the Oxford ring road, a van that had previously been used to break the strike when Murdoch moved his presses to Wapping. It still had the faded decals from his newspapers on the side panels, and some threatening black bumper bars. We screwed in sheets of plywood to partition us from the gear, and installed a clutch of old Rover car seats so we could hunker down on the long trips home.

A big moment in the day is sorting out the evening's set list. This is done by Ed, Thom and Phil, and can happen anywhere, from backstage catering to Japanese bullet trains. Jonny and I stay out of it. We're happy to play anything, in any order, so we're not much help. Lots of bands with big productions hardly change their set list, so as not to mess with the lighting and sound crew's song cues and set-up. We change a few songs most nights, to their mild consternation. It just feels more fun, more in tune with touring itself, breaking up the repetitive rhythm of playing all those anonymous arenas.

Soundcheck

Around 3 p.m., we take the stage at the Smoothie King arena, sidestepping the lighting crew who are focusing spots to where we will be standing. I'm always between two drum risers at the back, in front of my speaker cabinet, less distractingly laid on its side like a sofa of dub bass. Next to it is my SVT head amplifier, glowing with valves like dimly lit bulbs behind a sparkly silver screen. My two basses, a 1972 cream Fender Precision from a church band in Connecticut, and a battered 1963 sunburst Precision I bought with Nigel in Austin, Texas, are cradled in black stands. I have a pedal board for tuning and adding distortion, a sweet fuzz racket for some of the songs. I've only recently been allowed to have pedals on the floor, as I've occasionally trodden on them accidentally during some of the quieter songs.

Running through songs on theatre stages, spaces designed to project sound outwards, gives confidence and flight to your ideas. Soundcheck can be the best place to come up with new parts to songs, because of that performative edge you're given, the live kick of having to work instinctively, even if it's just to a handful of crew. It's like playing in a very expensive audio-visual rehearsal room, before the stress of an audience.

On previous nights, the vast auditoriums might have hosted sports teams: the New Orleans Pelicans perhaps, Miami Heat, Boston Celtics. Unlike old theatres, these multifunctional black boxes aren't haunted by past shows. At the beginning of it all, I would fall asleep at night dreaming about playing on a stage like Madison Square Garden. The stage is like a nest, a pulpit from where you peer out into the empty darkness. As you move from room to road to bus to car to plane and back to room again, strangely it becomes your one constant across the months of touring, the grey stage carpet travelling with you wherever you go. Everything on it is laid out in black and fluorescent strips of gaffer tape, X marking the spot where you are to stand.

When we're on stage, we're brought bottles of water, towels, electric guitars, cradled and cosseted, the crew walking deliberately and slowly, careful not to trip over cables or boxes. Flanked by two drummers, my body shakes with the sound, but my ears are capped off with an audio feed that separates everything and spares your hearing. With the warmth of that sofa dub behind me, I find myself luxuriating in my own intimate sound bath, hearing melody and rhythm combine.

Specialised in-ear monitors feed all the sounds you need to make sense of the songs. They have replaced the black monitors that used to squat at the front of the stage, inviting you to rest your foot on them in more impassioned musical moments. The in-ear monitors are individually moulded by the same Chicago company that looks after Formula 1 drivers and NASA's astronauts. They protect our ears from all the bang and fizz on stage, feeding us our own dedicated mixes from the wireless box gaffer-taped to our belts. The fancier ones have tiny microphones in them, so they can pick up the sound as it changes when you're moving about the stage – something, as a bassist, I'm not encouraged to do. My guitar tech, Adam, threatens me with a very short curly lead, like the ones used by The Clash back in the 1970s, that would keep me tethered to my spot.

It's important, especially for the singer, to be able to hear the crowd out front too, so audience ambience is bled into our in-ear mix (yes, they have mics too, and are part of the performance). Without it, playing a show can feel like being locked inside an anechoic box plunged deep on the ocean floor, with nobody there to witness us. It happened to us once at Leeds Festival. As the set progressed, Thom became convinced the 60,000 people out front had gone on some weird silent protest in the darkness. Later, we discovered that the Arctic Monkeys and Kings of Leon had endured something similar that same night in Reading. Thom thought he'd lost the crowd and was distraught, when he just couldn't hear them through his in-ears. The next night in Reading, we changed the set, the monitor engineer whacked up the audience microphones and Thom walked on stage, arms aloft like a game-show host heralding the start of the evening's fun.

Show

Playing live is a different set of nerves from the studio: the sea of arms and heads slowly dissolving in the evening light, or, if we're in a black-boxed arena, disappearing from us at the flick of a switch, leaving you feeling suddenly unmoored and alone, like unshot film in a camera's light-tight chamber. It's easier to accept the audience size if you can see it – wandering out onto a stage in near darkness, knowing they're out there somewhere, is much more alarming. Inspired by the first photography book I loved – Gaylord Oscar Herron's *Vagabond,* with its everyday shots of Kansas – I've tried to capture my experience of Radiohead crowds. There is a particular photograph in Herron's book of a small group of young people at what looks like a country festival. It's compelling because it both catches the collective energy of a mass of people and, as it freezes time and space, lets you encounter them individually: caught in the moment, lost in their own moments.

There's nothing you can do to dodge or delay the fear just before you walk on stage. Once you're out there, exposed, you learn to lose yourself in the music. Over time, I've taught myself to blot out the wobbles. Sometimes, usually near the start of the tour, if you are struggling, you find yourself analysing every fragment of sound as it's sent out, searching for any errors or lapses in synchronicity with the other bandmates. When it's working well, the music seems to meld and take on its own collective life. The song finished, you lift your head and gaze out at the crowd, and you aren't even conscious of having played it. It's as if the song has played itself and all we've done is helm a vast music box of light and sound. You are transported out of yourself, swept up into a surging wave of calm and euphoria, carried to a place of total communion with the crowd.

Festivals

Performing outdoors can sometimes feel ad hoc, but brings with it a sense of rawness, which is refreshing. There's less control over the space, and your lighting man is weeping because it doesn't get dark until 10 p.m. and you're on at 8. We've had flash floods in France, violent storms sweeping purple flight cases away in Buffalo Run, Virginia, and one time in San Diego, a missile from Bush's Star Wars tests streaked across the audience mid-set, lighting up the night sky, the only pyrotechnics we've ever had.

The first festival we played was Bevrijdings-pop in Haarlem, the Netherlands. *Bevrijdings* means 'liberation', and the small festival is part of the celebrations to commemorate the liberation of the Netherlands from Nazi tyranny on 5 May 1945. We were on second, in the middle of a sunny Wednesday afternoon, on a modest stage in a civic park with Haarlemers ambling past, eating ice creams and waffles, enjoying their national holiday. I have no memory of playing, other than the sight of people on sit-up-and-beg bikes gliding by the duck ponds and serried beds of orange and white tulips, and, later, the Dutch pop duo 2 Unlimited closing out the festival around dusk with their furiously optimistic hit 'No Limit'.

There's a sense of something pre-electric and almost primeval, especially if you are playing as the sun dips down. Time passes differently in the flow of music – it slows down and you can pick out the stars in the settling twilight as you stream sound and light across an open field of faces, freed from the ringing metallic echo of an arena's reverberation. At Coachella, the polo ground is so flat, the desert air so clear, that when the stage lights flare up they pour across the crowd like the full beams of a car in a crime movie. Within the golden canyon of Red Rocks, high up in the mountains of Colorado, the audience are perched on stone bleachers that rise up in front of the stage like a cliff. You can make out every single face, caught in the swirling stage lights, the crowd raked so steeply you feel that at any minute they might tumble into your lap on stage. There's the soft roar of fans who've climbed into the tree canopies that fringe the Greek Theatre in Los Angeles, fans again in the treetops at an extinct volcano outside Athens, the fat harvest moon that hung like a bloody egg as we played into the night above the Roman amphitheatre in Fréjus.

My favourite photographs of Ed were taken at Glastonbury, where he loves to go every year, whether or not we're playing. He adores the organised chaos of what, for four nights, becomes the third-largest city in the south-west of England. As a band, you're much more exposed, less in control, just a small part of the bill of entertainment for that seemingly endless midsummer's weekend. The crowds have been there long before you; you're there to join in the local pagan heritage. In those vast fields, with music lovers as far as the eye can see, huge tents and nightclubs glowing out of crashed planes, your performance is just a few short frames in a sprawling psychedelic movie of sound and light.

Glastonbury – a festival you are invited to play in a field by a farmer – bestows a unique musical humility which makes for a weird kind of pressure that no other gathering can match. Walking on stage in midsummer's dusty light or, once, in the dredging rain, is terrifying, because it means so much for me to be part of something that, like Jez Butterworth's play *Jerusalem*, celebrates an English idea of summer wildness, the illicit raves and eighties' gatherings I'd glimpsed as a teenager. When you manage to galvanise 100,000 revellers to sit tight and stay with you as the light falls, a strange hypnotic focus overwhelms you as the music ebbs and flows across the valley.

Exit Music

One of my other favourite photographs of Ed is of him just off the bus in Blackpool, waiting to get breakfast on the morning of 12 May 2006. We were playing songs from our future release, *In Rainbows*, and David Fricke from *Rolling Stone* had come up to write about us. We'd just driven from the Netherlands, perhaps via Oxford – I don't remember – and were due to play the beautiful Empress Ballroom, with its wide white arches, chandeliers that shook and glittered as we played, a wooden sprung floor that became another drum skin with the crowd dancing out a beat. Before all that, Ed's thousand-yard stare and bunk hair say leave me alone, at least until I've had coffee. In an image from that same tour, Jonny's plastic red suitcase explodes with crumpled denim and clothes. Another picture shows him holding a record he had just found in Blackpool, titled, prophetically, *Musique Rituelle – à travers temps et pays.* He's sitting in the top back lounge of a very ugly English tour bus, all upholstered in butterscotch and turquoise leatherette, a drinks table enmeshed in rubber anti-slip fabric you put under

rugs, for all those endless cups of tea slopping down the motorway home to Oxford.

There's a photograph of Thom with his hands held together in front of him – it's the end of the night, somewhere in America. I can't be sure where, because the image is so murky and the vast, blacked-out caverns are so similar. Let's say it's New Orleans' Smoothie King arena, 3 April 2017, around 11 p.m. We've finished our second encore, and Thom is here, thanking the 20,000 people out front. The white strip to Thom's left is his black-and-white Rhodes piano, wheeled on and off on a riser like a musical prop. I've stayed on stage while the others have drifted off, and I'm standing stage left, closer to Ed's microphone, to take in the image of Thom and the crowd.

The preceding two and a half hours were full of light and colour: acid blues, greens and yellows, the near ultraviolet purple that lends everything on stage an extra 3D glow. There are remote-controlled spotlights, cameras, multiple mirror balls, film projections from front of house onto a stage-wide silvery surfboard screen that is studded with thousands of light-emitting diodes. Thirty years ago, you could burn your leg on a floor lamp, and now the white-hot heat of technology runs cool, is pixelated, and fiercely bright. One day, this back screen will have more resolution and fidelity than the performers in front.

But at the end of the show, the stage lights go down, the house lights stay low, and we are finally left alone without our forcefield in front of all those people. They have their phones raised up, like cigarette lighters for the last power ballad. Their LEDs are lit this time, to help illuminate the sudden darkness as the audience record the scene. Many are live-streaming from their phones – thousands of one-person outside broadcast units for the web kids across the world and all its time zones. These haloed points of light throw up a weird phosphorescence, like creatures from the deep, hailing each other from inside the black belly of the Smoothie King, rippling up from the arena floor all the way to the nosebleed rake of the gods. In another sixty seconds, the house safety lights will flood this scene and wash it away, until it ebbs back, two nights later, at the Dunkin' Donuts Center.

For J, A and H, with love

Thank you to Nicholas Pearson,
Charlotte Robathan, Diana Talyanina,
Charlotte Cotton, Michael Mack,
Duncan Whyte and Ellie Pridgeon

First published in Great Britain in 2024
by John Murray [Publishers]

1

Editor: Nicholas Pearson
Edit and sequence: Colin Greenwood
and Duncan Whyte
Design: Duncan Whyte
Typefaces: JJannon, Simplon
Paper: 135 gsm Gardapat 13 Kiara,
120 gsm Magno Natural
Printed and bound in Italy by Graphicom S.p.A.

A CIP catalogue record for this title is
available from the British Library

Hardback ISBN 9781399817844
Special Edition ISBN 9781399817851
Deluxe Edition ISBN 9781399820950

John Murray policy is to use papers that are
natural, renewable and recyclable products
and made from wood grown in sustainable
forests. The logging and manufacturing processes are expected to conform to the environ-
mental regulations of the country of origin.

John Murray Press
Carmelite House
50 Victoria Embankment
London EC4Y 0DZ

www.johnmurraypress.co.uk

John Murray Press
part of Hodder & Stoughton Limited
An Hachette UK company